BOOK
OF
SONGS

KERRY LEE

NEWMAN SPRINGS PUBLISHING
320 Broad Street
Red Bank, NJ 07701

First originally published by Newman Springs Publishing 2024

ISBN 979-8-88763-914-7 (Paperback)
ISBN 979-8-88763-915-4 (Digital)

Printed in the United States of America

CONTENTS

Everything's good in Mama Mary's house. She took a fighter and turned him into a praiser. Enjoy everything placed before you in this table of contents.

In the House

When the atmosphere is set, praises are going up, Jesus is preparing
the way, Jesus, Jesus.

In the house (×2), on a Sunday morning, before the shouting
breaks out, the choir would raise up a standard of praise in the
atmosphere.
In the house (×2), early on a Sunday morning, hands and feet would
be making a sound.
In the house (×2), praises are going up, blessings down.
In the house, shouting out His name, Jesus, Jesus. Early on Sunday
morning, before the shouting breaks out, the choir would raise
up a standard of praise in the hearts of the saints.
In the house (×2), early on Sunday morning, before the shouting
break out.
In the house (×2), Jesus, Jesus, prepare the way in this house.
In the house (×3)

LET THE TRUMPET BLOW

Let the trumpet blow (×2), when I stand before the throne, I hope to hear God say, "My good and faithful servant, welcome home"
Let the trumpet blow (×2), my good and faithful servant, welcome home (×2), let the trumpet blow

When He separates the wheat from the chaff, I hope to hear God say, "My child, welcome home"

Let the trumpet blow (×2), when I use up my last breath here on earth, I hope to hear God say to me, "My good and faithful servant, welcome home"
Let the trumpet blow (×3), welcome home (×3)

I'M NOT UNARMED

Prophesize to yourself, "I'm not unarmed, I know Jesus, and He knows me"

When the storm kicks up, and it seems like the devil has caught you unarmed
I know Jesus (×2), and He knows me

The victory is already won, I know Jesus, and He knows me
I know Jesus (×2), so I can rest in the midst of a storm

When the storm kicks up, and it seems like the devil has caught you unarmed
I know Jesus (×2), and He knows me

I'm not unarmed (×2), even if I'm in the midst of a storm, remind yourself whom you belong to
I'm not unarmed (×3), I know Jesus, and He knows me
When you see a storm coming your way, prophesize to yourself, "I know Jesus, and He knows me, I'm not unarmed, I'm not unarmed (×3)

You Can't Stop the Rain

Hoping and wishing is not gonna change one thing, leave it in God's
hands

You can't stop the rain (×2), only God can, I know that God can

You can't stop the pain, you can't even wish it away, you can lay it in
Jesus's hands, just like an enemy opposing you
Put it in God's hands (×2)

You can take a stand, hoping and wishing is not gonna change one
thing
Yet God can, leave it in God's hands

You can't stop the rain (×2), only God can, I know that God can
He shuts up heaven, and nothing can come down

He can take away your pain and can let it rain down, blessing on you
each day
That's how good He is

Hoping and wishing is not gonna change one thing, leave it in God's
hands
You can't stop the rain (×2), only God can (×2)

Jesus Is What Makes It Right

There is a chamber you can enter when you drop down on your knees in prayer [2 Chronicles 7:14].

Oh, Jesus is what makes it right, He's bigger than day and night
Jesus is what makes it right if I have to wrestle all night
Jesus is what makes it right

He opens the door to my life, Jesus is what makes it right
He clears every devil out of my sight

Jesus is what makes it right, He's bigger than day and night
On my knees, I can cause the devil to flee
For greater is He that is in me than he that in the world [John 4:4]
He elevates my strength

Jesus is what makes it right, when I enter His chamber,
Jesus is what makes it right, Jesus is what makes it right

My Prayers Are Not Wasted

When I go down on my knees in prayer, my God will meet me there

My prayers are not wasted, when I send up my prayers one by one, I
    lay them in His hands, it's like releasing a dove in the air
One by one, I drop them in His hands

I can go out on limb, believing in Him, my prayers are not wasted on
    something I don't understand
I have no doubt my prayers went out, to the one who really cares

I sent up my prayers, like releasing a dove in the air
I know He will understand it by and by

My prayers are not wasted (×2), I know He's seen them one by one
I drop them in His hands, truly, I know Jesus has a plan

I will wait, I will wait, He holds time in His hands
My prayers are not wasted (×2), I will continue to go down on my
    knees in prayer
I know they are not wasted (×2)

I'm on My Journey

Each day that He lets me live, I'm taking a step, trying to get closer
     to Him

I'm on my journey (×2), I'm headed somewhere, with God's help, the
     kingdom of God in sight
With God's help, I can get there
I'm on my journey (×2), I been reading my road map, His holy Word
Rain or shine, God's presence will guide even if I was blind

A place called home, a place called heaven, a place full of love
Where I can be a part of celebrating the King on the throne

I'm on my journey (×2), I'm headed somewhere, with God's prom-
     ises, which are "Yes" and "Amen"
I can get there

I'm on my journey, when I get up there, the pearly gates will open up,
     and the angel will escort me in
I'm on my journey, I'm on my journey to stand before the King
Trumpets blowing, praising, going on with a number of saints
Who have made this journey home
I'm on my journey (×3)

STANDING ROOM ONLY

Every soul going home, good or bad, will stand before the King on
the throne

I'm ready to get my praise on, celebrating the King on the throne
Standing room only (×2)

Imagine you are standing before the King of glory
My Master reigns (×3), the only thing you can do is give Him praise
My Master reigns (×3), standing room only, standing room only

Angels hover over the throne, singing, "Hallelujah, hallelujah"
Standing room only, standing room only

Giving praises to the Creator, my Master reigns (×3)

I'm ready (×3), to get my praise on

Only hellfire will be given to the ones who were caught in the wrong

Standing room only (×3), my Master reigns (×2)

Jesus Came

When He already is the I Am that I Am with, everything revolves
    around His plan

Jesus can claim us (×2), He offered up His life
If only we would trust Him (×2), our living would not be in vain

Jesus came (×2), the God that's more than enough, that you can
    always trust

Jesus came (×2), so that you can live and learn
He holds all creation power in His hands

Jesus can claim us (×2), yet He would rather that we claim Him
For who He is (×2)

Surely, if you know the keeper of your soul, our living would not be
    in vain

Jesus can claim, Jesus can claim everything, 'cause everything revolves
    around His plan

When He is already the I Am that I Am
Jesus came (×3), I Am that I Am (×3)

OH GOD, SHIELD ME

Every day I put my trust in the Lord, His shield stretches over this
    whole wide world

Oh, thank You, Lord (×2), for You shield me from unseen and seen
    danger
Until my faith catches up, keep me under Your shield

Oh God, shield me (×2) from seen and unseen danger
I know You can, Lord (×2), keep me in Your hands

Oh, shield me, I know that You can, Lord
Enroll me in Your witness protection plan

Oh, thank You, Lord (×2), for You shield me from unseen and seen
    danger
This is my request, keep on loving me
I truly need Your help
Oh God, shield me (×2), from unseen and seen danger
Oh, shield me (×3)

JESUS, MY ALL AND ALL

I don't mind sharing a word that can free up your soul
I strongly recommend Jesus (×3), if you are weary or wounded
Weary, weary, weary, or wounded and sad

I strongly recommend Jesus (×3), if He can't fix it, nobody can
If you have been abandoned by this world
I strongly recommend Jesus (×3), a very good friend
Hungry for joy and my burdens are weighing me down

I strongly recommend Jesus (×3), Jesus, my all and all
Oh, He will work it out
If I'm hungry for joy and my burdens are weighing me down

I strongly recommend Jesus (×3), He is my all and all

An echo from my past would say to me, "Talk to Jesus and tell Him
    all about you troubles, He will work it out"
Jesus, my all and all (×3)

ALL ABOARD

September 15, 2022

I don't know my final stop in the Lord, I just hope I'm aboard
When it's time to go home, I want to hear my Savior say, "My good
    and faithful servant"

All aboard (×2), let's go home
When this life is over, and this soul has no more earthly vessel
I want to hear, "Come on up here, my good and faithful servant"
The spirit of Lord is guiding me home

All aboard (×2), climb the stairway to heaven
"Come up, my good and faithful servant"
My final stop is home in glory
"Well done, my good and faithful servant" (×2)
When this life is over, and this soul has no more earthly vessel

All aboard (×2)

GET UP, SAINTS

Fill up this house with praise, reach out to the Lord on this day, a day
of praise, even if you have to fall on your face
Giving praise, giving Him praise

Get up, get up, saints, let us all magnify His name, thank Him, thank
Him in your praise, feed off your soul, while going after the
Holy Ghost

Dance, dance, dance, give Him praise, break up any sad, sad face, let
us magnify His name

Get up, saints (×2), renew your faith, thank Him (×2), in your praise

He is worthy to be praised (×2), get up, saints (×3)

Reach out to the Lord on this day, create in you a sacred place
Where the Lord can meet you every day

Get up, saints, let us magnify His name, oh, let us thank Him for
His saving grace
Get up, saints (×3)

HE RESERVED A PLACE FOR ME

I can count it, all joy, when I add it all up, Jesus is the VIP who stayed there and wouldn't come down.

I'm in a shouting mood, He wouldn't come down (×2)
Then He reserved a place for me in His father's house, in His's father house

I'm in a mood, my Savior has spoken, my Savior has spoken
I'm in a shouting mood, Jesus, I love you, my VIP

My VIP, reserve a place for me
I watch my burdens fall down (×2), the chain fell off (×2)
Jesus is my VIP who stayed there and wouldn't come down
When He did, He went on to His father's house
He reserved a place for me
I can count it, all joy, when I add it all up

THE CONTROLLER OF MY FAITH

Seek His face and pray, and He will guide you with His amazing
grace

Guide me, Lord (×2), the controller of my faith
I've got a confession to make, I'm nothing without Jesus

He's my regulator, without Him, I'm out of control
I've got a confession to make, I'm nothing, nothing without Jesus

The controller of my faith, He controls my night, He controls my
day

I've got a confession to make, I'm nothing without Jesus
The controller of faith, guide me, Lord, the controller of my faith

IN THE PRESENCE OF THE LORD

Go in and seek His face, kneel down, and pray

There is a chamber I can go in to kneel down and pray

In the presence of the Lord (×2)

The chamber of grace (×2)

In the present of the Lord (×2)

The chamber of mercy (×2)

In the presence of the Lord (×2)

I can go in and kneel down and pray

There is a chamber I can go in to kneel down and pray
My heavenly Father, won't turn me a way
He's always there (×2)

Under the Cloud of Rest

September 11, 2022

Your storm in your life may have been going on for some time now,
    when you know the peacemaker, you can surely rest

Under this cloud of rest, for my Savior reigns (×2)
I confess
Under this cloud, I rest in peace (×2)
How much more will He share with me?
Under this cloud of rest
A double portion of joy you lost will return unto you
When I worship Him, when darkness falls (×2), I embrace His rest
I won't let darkness alarm my rest
Under the cloud of rest (×2), I will fear no evil, for Jesus already said
    it best, peace, be still (×2)
He surely is the peace maker
My Savior reigns (×2)

Unbreakable Love (God, Do What You Do)

Unbreakable love (×2)
God, I surrender to You, all my burden, do what You do (×2)
Unbreakable love (×2), wash my sin away (×2)
You hold the world in Your hands
Unbreakable love, unbreakable
Do what You do (×2), forgive, forgive me of my sin
Unbreakable love (×2)

God, do what You do, do what You do
You redeem us of our sin
God, I surrender to Your will (×2)
I surrender to You (×2)
Unbreakable love (×2)

I ARM MYSELF

Sometime you find yourself alone, without anybody's help, you got to put on the garment of praise.

I arm myself (×2), with the weapon of praise, when I'm attacked and
    I don't have help from anybody else
I put on the garment of praise, it shields me, it covers me
I arm myself (×2), in God's Word with the weapon of praise
I've been out here on the battlefield all by myself
I arm myself (×2), with the weapon of praise
When I'm attacked and I don't have help from anybody else
Lord, You are my refuge in times of distress
I know You're always there
I arm myself (×2), with the weapon of praise
I put on the garment of praise
I arm myself (×2), with the weapon of praise

I Need Him to Live

When you come to the conclusion in your heart that you just can't make it without Jesus.

I can't (×2), I just can't break the chain, that binds me to Him
Nothing can live without Him
The God that keeps on giving that I may live
I know that there is power in Jesus, so I can't, I just can't, I just can't
    live without Him
I need Him so I can live, I can't, you know I just can't break the chain
That chain, oh, that chain, that binds me to Him
Nothing can live without Him, before His Word fails nothing will
    exit

I need Him (×3), so I can live

I'm Going after Jesus

I committed myself to follow Jesus, no turning back

If there is a turn I should have taken, help me, Lord, get back on the
right track

I'm going after Jesus (×2)

If there a turn I should have taken, turn me to Jesus (×2), the true
and living vine, He will give me peace of mind

The true and living vine (×2)
I'm going after Jesus, He will wrap his arms around me, and carry me
higher, His love is a sustaining power

If there is a turn I should have taken, help me, Lord, get back on the
right road, turn me around (×2)
Place my feet back on solid ground

I'm going after Jesus (×3)

LORD, I THANK YOU

Lord, You've been mighty good to me over the years, and nobody can
do the work that You do

Lord, I thank You (×2), for the many signs so that life won't leave me
behind

You place me in this moment of time, where life just won't leave me
behind

I thank You (×2), I'm grateful, for why I'm still living today

I'm thankful for all my help that comes from above, I thank You, for
this strength, oh, what a special gift to end up with

Lord, I thank You (×2), for these signs so that life won't leave me
behind

Lord, I thank You for the many signs and wonders that life let me
walk into
Even the change of time doesn't leave me behind
Lord, I thank You (×3)

OH, OKAY, LORD

When you are dealing with an ounce of faith
Your trust issues are so far away, I will step out on an ounce of faith

Somehow You touch me (×2), somehow I believe You will show me
    the way

Oh, okay, Lord (×2)
I will walk by faith, even though I'm dealing with an ounce of faith

Oh, okay, Lord (×2)
I believe You, Lord (×2), mountains have to move out of my way

Oh, okay, Lord (×2)
I'm dealing with an ounce of faith, even though, I don't see the way
Oh, okay, Lord (×3)

I Need Help (Turning This Love Around)!

I don't want her, I don't want her to be just a memory in time
I need help! (×3)
Turning this love around, each step she takes away from me, my
    heart falls to the ground
I need help! (×3)
Turning this love around

I don't want her to just to be a memory in time
I need help! (×3)
My heart is racing throughout my mind
I need help!
Turning this love of mine in reverse
Oh, what have I done, it's gonna put me six feet underground
This woman that I love is gonna put me six feet underground
Turn her around (×3), this love of mine

Your Grace Is Sufficient

When I have done all I can, I will hold on to your word

Your word in my ears (×2), nothing is in vain (×2), when you call
    His name

Nothing is in vain (×2), when your trials have been replaced

Situation after situation, make me call out Jesus's name
Your word in my ears, your grace is sufficient

Nothing is in vain, when I call His name

You in my ears (×2), your prayers are not in vain when you call out
    His name

Jesus, Jesus, there is power in His name, nothing is like His power,
    you can claim victory in His name
Your word in my ears (×2), your grace is sufficient
Situation after situation, make me call out Jesus name
Your word in my ears (×3)

You Got My Water Running

When You love on me, I get filled up inside, then my tears start running down

Each time You love on me, I get fill up inside
I'm a person with pride (×2), when You love on me, You turn my world upside down
You got my water running (×2), each time You love on me

My tears of joy overflow in my heart
I tell You my water's running
I'm a person of pride (×2), you place a word in my mind, surely, I can't deny

Each time You love on me, Lord, You get my water running deep down inside

Each time You love on me, I get filled up inside, then my tears start running down
A person with a whole lot of pride (×2), my tears of joy overflow in my heart
You got my water running (×3), when You love on me

OH JESUS

Your Word keeps on producing each time I reach out to You

Oh Jesus, You multiply my grace, each time I reach out to You, You got grace that increases my faith

Each time I reach out to You, You supply me with grace that increases my faith

Oh Jesus, You always make a way, Your Word keeps on building, something inside

There is always something new being produced when I keep close to You

Oh Jesus, You multiply my grace, each time I reach out to You, You got grace that increases my faith

Oh Jesus, You always make a way, Your Word keeps on building, something inside, I know I can try when I can keep my eyes on my supplier

Your Word keeps on producing (×2)

ARE YOU AFRAID

Sometimes you have to ask yourself if you are afraid of the condition you find yourself in. Remember the one who sits high and looks low (Matthew 6:24).

Are you afraid (×2), to call His name?
Raise your voice, it's not hard standing on who you know

Are you afraid (×2), to call His name, the name above all names, the name demons are afraid to entertain?

Oh, He loves you (×2), don't you know that He saves the lost every day?

Are you afraid to give Him praise?
Are you afraid to say His name?
Yes, He's a healer, yes, He's a deliverer, Jesus is His name, yes, He's the one that pardons us of our sins

Say it when you wake up, say it when you lie down
You will hate one and love the other

LET THE RECORD SHOW

Can you see the glory in His word? Even the demon said, "I know
who You are"

What evidence do you have, that you woke yourself up?
What evident do you have? Let us compare, let us compare

Let the record show, the life-giving God I know, surely, He loves us so

Can you breathe without Him?
Can you see without Him?
Let us compare (×2)

Can a physician heal thyself? We all need God's help
He separated night from day, He raises the sun up in morning

Let us compare (×2)
Let the record show, the life-giving God I know, surely, He loves us so

Jesus Remains the Same

Today, tomorrow, and evermore
He just won't change, for He already finished what He started at the
    beginning

He can point to the beginning, when He said, "Let us make man"

Jesus just won't change, He just remains the same
He saw everything He said, He was sure of Himself

No need to complain, Jesus remains the same
We've just got to walk it out (×2)

We just need to know God's got everything in His control
In Him, His Word, still the same, today, tomorrow, and evermore

He can point to the beginning, when He said, "Let us make man"

He holds the power (×2), for He has the plan
Jesus remains the same (×3)

JESUS

Jesus, Jesus, Jesus, the name that drives the devil insane, Jesus
Jesus, Jesus, Jesus, when I think about You, I count it all good
It's good (×2), to be covered by You
Jesus, Jesus, You're all good
I can count it all good
Jesus, Jesus, when I think about You
I count it all good
Your name just assured me
I can count it all good
It's good, it's good to be covered by You
When Your love ran down as blood
Jesus, Jesus, I count it all good

CROSSING OVER

Crossing over (×2), oh, walk on (×2)
Your journey won't be long, when your head's up yonder, you've got
    a crossing to make (×2)
You're going on up to heaven's gate
Crossing over (×2)
You've got a crossing to make (×2)
Oh, walk on (×2)

When the angel announces your arrival with the trumpet's sound
You've got a crossing to make (×2), oh, walk on (×2)
Crossing over (×2)
No more crying, no more dying
Oh, walk on (×2)
When your head's up yonder, where we're gonna crown Him
Oh, walk on (×2)
Crossing over (×2)

EMMANUEL

The story was told a long time ago, God with us (×2)
After the three wise men followed a shining star, that rested over
     Bethlehem, they knelt down beside Emmanuel
God with us (×2)

As the three wise men, worshipped Him
Emmanuel, Emmanuel, God with us (×2)

I don't know how long, yet the record, recorded was said the star was
     observed over seventy days

God with us (×2)

He will protect us, He will save us
Now we worship Him
Emmanuel, Emmanuel, God with us (×2), day by day (×2), eternity
     is in His hand

I Can't Believe It

His love up lifted me in more ways than one
He caught me off guard, He is the Way, the Truth, and the Life

He called me His son, I can't believe it (×2), my victory has already
    been won

He called me His son (×3). He claimed me as His son. He talked to
    me as if I am His son

I can't believe it (×2), He called me His son
He called me His son, while holding me in His arms

I can't believe it (×2), when this world calls me less than a child of
    God, He called me His son
He said unto me, "I am the Way, the Truth, and the Life"

Hey, Mama

I got something to talk to you about, Mama
There is something I need to know

Hey, Mama (×2), Santa and his reindeer
Are about to fly, and I haven't seen one drop of
Snow on the tops, not even on the ground

Hey, Mama (×2), is Santa going to drop by?
Hey, Mama (×2), is Santa gong to drop by?

The sky is clear, no snow has appeared
Please check the weatherman

Hey, Mama (×2), it's the season for Santa to drop by

I haven't seen one drop of snow on the rooftops
Not even on the ground

Hey, Mama (×2), is Santa going to stop by?
Hey, Mama (×3)

Mary Lee Davis/Mom

I Wanna Share with You

I know some of you brought your doom and gloom in the house
   with you, dropping them in the collection basket and offering
   them up to Jesus

What you offer up to Him, don't take it back
I can share with you that God is good
What He really wants is your heart
I wanna share that with you (×2)
What you offer up to Him, don't you take it back
I wanna share that with you (×2), give Him your heart, place your
   offering in the collection basket, and offer them up to Jesus
What you offer up to Him, don't take it back, don't take your trouble
   with you
I wanna share that with you, God is good
What you offer up to Him, don't take it back
Praise Him with your whole heart, He deserves it
He deserves it

CAN'T KEEP MY MOUTH SHUT

My mouth, my hands, and my feet just wanna celebrate the King
I can't keep my mouth shut

I can't keep my mouth shut (×2), Lord, You've been too good

Can't keep my mouth shut (×2), You've been too good

My hands and my feet remind me of just what I need
So I can't keep my mouth shut, can't keep my mouth shut

You set my soul on fire, can't hold back my praise

You've been too good (×2), can't sit down, can't control my feet

Can't keep my mouth shut (×2), You've been too good, Lord, You've
    been too good

My mouth, my hands, and my feet just wanna celebrate the King
Can't keep my mouth shut

WELL, WELL, WELL

When God steps in, He washes away my tears, that's how good He is

My crying didn't have the power to put out the fire that was burning
    inside
Well, well, well, then came down my help in the form of a shower

My crying didn't have the power to turn around my trial
I went down on my knees and reached out to the almighty King
Well, well, well, then my love came down with my help
Well, well, well

Then the rain came down, my tears disappeared

My crying didn't have the power that it once did, 'cause Jesus stepped
    in, and took away my tears

My crying didn't have the power it once did, when God stepped in
Well, well, well (×2)

A Siren Going Off

When you hear something in your spirit to
Warned you an intruder is on your grounds

There is a siren going off in my spirit
To warn me, "An enemy is on the grounds"

I've got security with God (×2), there is an angel watching over me

There is a siren going off (×2)
In my spirit, I'm alert 'cause
A siren's going off

I've got security with my Lord (×2)

A siren going off (×2)
An enemy on my grounds, I'm covered by Jesus
Blood, I've got help from above

God releases an angel to recover my loss
I've got security with God (×2)

LOVE OF MY LIFE

WALKING IN A DANGER ZONE

When you've been hanging too long, around the wrong soul
There is danger when you don't know when to go home
Sin, sin, will turn you in, when you are walking in a danger zone
You will in up walking alone, walking in a danger zone
Sin, sin, will turn you in, when you are walking in a danger zone
Your spirit and your flesh may just cause you to fail your test
Sin, sin, will turn you in, like walking in a wonderland
When your soul cries out for help, you are walking in a danger zone
    (×2)

I'M FIRED UP

When something rests in your heart and you are in a moment, you
     just can't stop
I'm fired up (×2), all I wanna do is talk about my Savior
I'm fired up (×2), my soul's got me worked up, when Jesus showed
     up, He brought me peace
Just what I needed, He brought me joy, just what I needed
I'm fired up (×2), all I wanna do is talk about my Savior
A very good friend of mine
I'm fired up (×2), my shoes have got to hold up (×2), my spirit is on
     fire (×2)
Lord, help me as I reach out to You
I'm fired up (×2)
The way He touched me

Wait for It

December 22, 2022

Peace, be still (×2), wait on the Lord
Wait for it (×2), your change is gonna come
Wait for it (×2), it's gonna move in like a storm
Everything not tied down will be tossed around
Wait for it (×2), your change is gonna come, it's gonna move in like
    a storm
What in the world is going on? Wait for it (×2)
He's gonna take your heart by storm
Your mind is gonna say, "What's going on?"
Wait for it (×2)
Your change is gonna come, peace, be still (×2), wait for it (×3)

IF I COULD FLY

When someone enters your world and keeps moving on

Oh, fly, girl, I would love to add you to my route
If I could fly, girl, you know I would be coming by
Oh, fly, girl, you enter my world
Oh, fly, girl, you enter my world, the way you make me feel so good
    inside

I would love to hang around, I would always hang around
You are the best thing in town

If I could fly, girl, you know I would be coming by, I would be hang-
    ing on the power lines

If I could fly, girl, I would add you to my route
Oh, fly, girl, you enter my world, now I'm in love

I wanna add you to my route

I'VE GOT TO STOP DOING THAT

I'm blocking my own blessing, I need to knock the chip off my
    shoulder

I've got to stop doing that, I'm going to knock the chip off my own
    shoulder (×2)
Letting my fault get the best of me

I've got to stop doing that (×2), I'm blocking my own blessing
I'm going to stop doing that

I'm going to stop standing in the Lord's way
I'm going to stop standing in the way
I'm blocking my own blessing (×2)

I've got to stop doing that, I'm going to knock the chip off my own
    shoulder (×2)
I'm blocking my own blessing (×2)
Letting my fault get the best of me

My Lord, help me, please, I'm blocking my own blessing (×2)
I've got to stop doing that (×3)

STANDING AT THE CROSSROADS (MY SAFETY IS IN JESUS CHRIST)

Standing at the crossroads (×2)
Trying to figure out which way I should go
Standing at the crossroads, which way will serve me so?
Standing at the cross, and life tells me I can go
Yet which is to the throne?
Standing at the crossroads, Lord, direct me home
Standing at the cross, standing at the crossroads
Surely, I can go
My safety is in Jesus Christ
Standing at the crossroads (×2)
Trying to figure out which way I should go
Standing in the crossroads (×2)

He Let Me Look In

This is a mighty good place to be, any moment where God wants to
reveal Himself

He let me look in (×3), for a moment (×2), I believe I've been set free,
from all of life that has been troubling me

For God has granted me, liberty to see beyond all that I can't see

For a moment now (×2), my joy has been pouring down

He let me look in (×3), I'm overjoyed, what God has granted me, a
moment of liberty with all of heaven serenading the King

I'm going home (×2), for a moment (×2), where there is joy all around
the throne

He let me look in (×3)

WHEN JUDGEMENT STOPS BY

Saints, you've got to know Jesus is an on-time God (Hezekiah 2, Kings 20:5–6).

When judgement stops by, Jesus steps in and renews my time
Joy was released in my heart, judgement made his demand
Yet God had other plans

When judgement stops by (×2), Jesus steps in and renews my time
My God can change things for my good

When judgement stops by (×2), Jesus steps in and renews my time

Joy was released in my heart, grace stood in and renewed my time
Judgement made his demand, my God had other plans

When judgement stops by (×2), Jesus steps in and renews my time,
    and that's what made all the difference
When judgement stops by (×2)

You Didn't Pass Me By

I've got a whole lot of reasons to give You praise, if I had to number them, you would say, "Just give praise," for He didn't pass you by

I've been there before (×2)
You didn't pass me by
There were days I wanted to just give up
I've been there before (×2), yet God wouldn't let me go, been there before (×2)

Lord, You didn't pass me by, You told me, "I will be by your side"
Now I can smile (×2)

I cried out to the Lord, "I thank You for not passing me by"

Mercy showed up on time, You didn't pass me by
Peace showed up on time, Lord, You relieve the pressure on my mind

In greater struggle, You didn't pass me by
I've been there before (×2)
Your love just wouldn't let me go

Running from My Past

DGG, Drugs, Guns, and Gangs

We all have a past that we are not proud of in some shape or form
We would love to put it to rest

Running from my past (×2), I'm not proud, I just want to let go, of
　　all the madness that wanted to put me in a hole
Running from my past (×2), those streets wanted to claim me, but I
　　didn't let go
Running from my past (×2), bloodstains on the grass, danger
　　everywhere
Running from my past, many mothers end up so sad
I just want to let go, of all the madness that wanted to put me in a
　　hole
The jail calls out, the grave calls out, who will be next?
I tell you, I'm running from my past
Running from my past (×3)
DGG, Drugs, Guns, and Gangs

ROCK THE MOUNTAIN

You don't have to put up with an adversary, turn him over to Master
He will send a shock wave unto his heart
Shock wave of praise (×2)
I'm gonna rock the mountain and cause a land of praise
I wanna rock the mountain, sending up praise
I'm gonna praise Him when the sun comes up
I'm gonna praise Him when the sun goes down

I'm gonna keep on praising Him until my adversary is shaking, trem-
    bling in fear

Shock of praise (×2)

I'm gonna rock the mountain and cause a landslide with my praise
I'm gonna rock the mountain (×2), with my praise
I know my Father's up there, so I'm gonna rock the mountain with
    my praise

JESUS, YOU SET THE STANDARD

You taught us how to love one another as thyself
Lord, You walk the walk that You taught

Oh, where would I be without Jesus on my side?
Jesus, You set standard, for my life (×2)
Oh, help me walk right, let Your Word fill me up inside

Jesus, You set the standard (×2), how I should live my life
Jesus, You are my teacher (×2), You help me walk right
I'm being blessed when I walk right, You bless me when I walk right

Jesus, You set the standard (×2), how I should live my life
This old building cannot stand without Christ
Oh, where would I be, if I let this world set the standard for me?
Jesus, You set the standard (×3)

WHEN THE SPIRIT OF THE LORD SENDS YOU

Sometimes you have to knock on doors, and stand in corners to do
the will of the Lord
Just tell yourself, "I'm on a mission"

Knock, knock, knock, knock

I'm on a mission (×2), to spread God's Word all over this land
To meet every soul, I'm on a mission to spread the kingdom to every
living soul
Knock, knock, knock, knock

If you have ears to hear, with a mind that wants to know, who is rich
in mercy, that's seated on the throne

I'm on a mission, to spread the kingdom to every living soul
Yes, God is on the throne, He's seated on the throne
Knock, knock, knock, knock

When the spirit of the Lord sends me, I'm on a mission, knock,
knock, knock, knock

GUIDE ME, OH LORD

Sometimes we are caught up in a crowd, and we can't figure which
    way to turn

Lord, let Your spirit be my guide (×2), no greater love, I can't deny

Guide me, oh Lord (×2), the all-seeing God

Your will (×2), let it be done
Lord, let Your spirit be my guide (×2)
Continue to turn me inside out

You can take a crowd in the midst of a dark night, and lead them to
    victory

The only crowd I wanna be caught up in, is the one You're leading
    me in

Oh, guide me, oh Lord (×2), no greater love, I can't deny
Let Your spirit be my guide, let Your spirit turn me inside out
Nobody greater (×2)

He Saw Me

When God said in the beginning, "Let us make man," He saw me

What Jesus saw while hanging on the cross
He saw me (×3), His love wouldn't let Him come down, to save His
    own life
His mission so much greater, He let His blood be the key to wash all
    my sins away
He saw me (×3), while pinned on the cross

He saw me (×3), His love wouldn't let Him come down, to save His
    own life
What He saw (×2), He saw me, from heaven, He decided to be the
    living sacrifice
He saw me (×3), He let his blood be the key to wash all my sins away

YOUR POWER BEING DISPLAYED

Lord, we marvel over how great You are, let Your light shine so bright

Your power being displayed (×2), oh, let me stand up in Your grace
Your power being on display (×2), healing taking place
Oh, let Your light so shine, forgiveness is taking place
Your power is being displayed (×2), oh, let me stand up in Your grace
Your power is being displayed. Can this house say hallelujah? Say
    hallelujah! Say hallelujah!
Lord, Your love fills up this place
Your power being displayed, Your power is on display

There is grace in this place, there is mercy in this place
Lord, we marvel over how great You are, let Your light shine so bright

CHILD OF GOD

I'm a child of God that's got praise building up in his heart, for the
love of God.

A child of God (×2), who He loves with all His heart.
Every bone in this body wants to get praise going on.

A child of God (×2), who loves Jesus with all his heart.
I am building up inside, my feet speaking to me, "Let me go free."

I'm a child of God (×2), that's got praise building up inside

I'm about to have a hallelujah good time. I'm a child of God, who's
got praise building up inside.
I'm about to have a good time, oh, this child of God.

THY KINGDOM COME

In this life, I will swing and miss sometimes, yet I've still got to walk
   this course

I gotta walk (×2), I gotta line up my talk

I gotta line up with His Word
Thy kingdom come, deliverance is my reward

I gotta walk this course, I gotta walk (×2)
I gotta line up with His Word, I wanna win His heart
Thy kingdom come (×2), deliverance is my reward
I gotta line up, and I gotta walk, I wanna win His heart, and be
   invited to the Promised Land

Thy kingdom come, Thy will be done (×2), deliverance is my reward
I gotta walk (×2)

I wish to play on the hill and in the valley
Thy kingdom come (×2)
He causes me to shout for joy

I gotta walk (×2), I gotta talk, with my Savior divine
Thy kingdom come (×2), deliverance is my reward

CAMEO APPEARANCE
(LOVE, LOVE, LOVE)

December 16, 2019

Love, love, love, love (×2), girl, I found myself so in love with you
I'm just a shadow that wants to walk with you, I wanna love you

I know that you are tied to another, if only you could see into my
        dreams, just how you've been walking with me
Love, love, love, love (×2)
Girl, I found myself so in love with you
My dream girl (×2)
You control my world

I'm just a shadow that wants to walk you, I wanna love you
I know that you are tied to another
Love, love, love, love (×2)
I need heaven above to see you my way

Love, love, love, love (×2)

FOR YOU AND ME

Turn to your neighbor and say, "You hold special access to Jesus, for
    He hung on in there, just for you and me"

For you and me (×2), you hold special access to Jesus who hung on
    the cross
Hold my hands (×2), hold my hands tight, even when you cried out
    loud, "Father, Father, forgive them, for they no not what they
    do"

For you and me (×2), you hold special access to Jesus, who hung on
    the cross
To save us, He wouldn't come down
Hold my hands (×2), hold my hands tight
You hold special access to Jesus, who hung on the cross

He gave up so we may live, He took on our sin
For you and me (×2), that's what love is, He gave up so you and I
    may live
For you and me (×3)

I Know the Fixer

Jesus is never too late, for His eyes, are always ahead of my time
He calls me His child
He can make it all good

I know the fixer (×2), of my faith
I may be broken, I may be worn out
I can call on my, my interceder, He can make rearrangements of my
    situation, and make me all good

I know the fixer (×2), of my faith
My interceder gives me grace
He knows when I'm broken, I may be worn out, I may drag along for
    a while, yet He's still on time

He shows me mercy, He shows me grace, I know the fixer (×2)
My Lord, my Lord, knows how to fix me when I'm broken
My, my, interceder can make rearrangements to fix my situation
He can make me all go
I know the fixer (×2)

I'VE SEEN HIM WITH
MY OWN EYES

November 11, 2022

With my own eyes (×2), I've seen Him high and lifted up
My soul took me to the mountaintop, to see my Savior on the cross
It took power to stay there, it took love to stay there, my precious
    Savior

To come down was not an option, He was committed to hanging on
    there

With my own eyes (×2), my soul took me to the mountaintop
To see my Savior on the cross

He was high and lifted up
He was committed to paying the ultimate sacrifice, for all human life

My soul took me to the mountaintop, to see my Savior on the cross,
    yet the good news was He wouldn't stay there

I've seen Him (×2), with my own eyes, He was high and lifted up
    with a crown of thorns on His head

Goo, Goo, Goo, Goo

God loves to see His child smile at Him
And make all kinds of noises when that special one shows up in His
   face

In God's eyesight, I will always be His child, that breaks out into a
   smile
"Goo, goo, goo, goo," is interpreted as "Father, I love you, goo, goo,
   goo, goo"

He interprets my "goo, goo, goo" and smile as a child, my heart beats
   with a smile, if you know how it feels playing with a little child
Their smile and "goo, goo" turn your world upside down

God loves to see His child kicking his feet up and down, with a big,
   oh, smile, "Goo, goo, goo, goo" is interpreted as "Father, I love
   you, I love you"

GOD KNOWS YOU'VE GOT AN ENEMY

He is going to and fro, seeking whom he may devour [1 Peter 5:8]

God knows you've got an enemy looking over your shoulder, waiting
for the right moment

To persuade you, ready to guide you, with that curious mind

Don't lose your focus and be persuaded on what looks good

God knows you've got an enemy who is out there, seeking whom he
may devour

God's got redeeming power greater than the devil's influencing power
That's what His love does when He sends His love down from above

He is ready to use His redeeming power, when you call out, "Father,
Father, I have fallen, and I can't get up on my own"

God knows you've got an enemy looking over your shoulder (×3)

HEALING AND DELIVERANCE

When God set you free, you are free indeed

Say to yourself, "I'm on my way out" [Daniel 6:22]

I got a wake-up call
Healing and deliverance (×3)
I know He can bring me out of my lion's den
I had the luxury of knowing Jesus at an early age, hanging around
    saints who have endured their pain
Healing and deliverance (×2), they had a testimony that would cause
    you to dance all day
Healing and deliverance (×2)
If He's done it for them, I know He can bring me out of my lion's den
When you are seeking out a friend, in the midst of the lion's den,
    Jesus walks in
Healing and deliverance (×3)

TRUST IN THE LORD

Trust in Lord like how the sheep always listen for their master's voice
Stand by (×2), God knows your heart's desire
Trust in Lord, wipe those tears from your eyes
Stand by (×2), God knows your heart's desire
Trust in Lord, trust in the Lord
He is the God who can turn back the hands of time
Stand by (×2), and witness God's mighty hands, that will overtake
    the hands of time
Stand by (×2), God knows your heart's desire
Trust in the Lord (×2)
He will rescue you in time, stand by (×2), God knows your heart's
    desire
Even from the beginning, so wipe those tears from your eyes
Trust in the Lord, and stand by (×3)

Meemaw

Grandma loves Aydah Grace
Meemaw (×2), Meemaw (×2), I popped the bubble (×2)
Meemaw (×2), Meemaw (×2), I popped the bubble (×2)
Playing outside, just having a good time, with my meemaw
I popped the bubbles, some went up, some went down, me and my
    meemaw having a good time
Now I'm looking down from heaven, watching the balloons coming
    up
I enjoyed my time with my meemaw, I never want to go back to one
    of my earthly homes, unless I get to stay with my meemaw
From heaven I watch the balloons coming up, Meemaw, I popped
    the balloons, Meemaw, Meemaw I so love you

Baby Picture

In Memory of Aydah Grace 2018-2021

ABOUT THE AUTHOR

Brother Kerry T. Lee attended Providence Christian Ministry in Birmingham, Alabama. He is a devoted father and husband who graduated from Phillips High, in the city of Birmingham. He is a security guard who has been stationed at ABC Coke in Tarrant City, Alabama from 2019 up to now.

Brother Lee came up in church, singing by his mother Mrs. Mary L. Davis's side. As a man now, he writes songs that come into his heart. He is one of only five siblings out of seven, along with Mattie, Patricia, Sandra, and Jeffere. He took up writing songs with the help of a coworker name Clyde Walton, who guides him on.